W9-CCA-780

GREAT MINDS OF SCIENCE

Stephen Hawking

Breaking the Boundaries of Time and Space

John Bankston

Enslow Publishers, Inc.

40 Industrial Road   PO Box 38
Box 398   Aldershot
Berkeley Heights, NJ 07922 Hants GU12 6BP
USA   UK

http://www.enslow.com

Copyright © 2005 by John Bankston

All rights reserved.

No part of this book may be reproduced by any means
without the written permission of the publisher.

Library of Congress Cataloging-in-Publication Data

Bankston, John, 1974-
Stephen Hawking : breaking the boundaries of time and
space / John Bankston.
p. cm. — (Great minds of science)
Includes bibliographical references and index.
ISBN-10: 0-7660-2281-1
1. Hawking, S. W. (Stephen W.)—Juvenile literature. 2. Physicists—
Great Britain—Biography—Juvenile literature. 3. Big bang theory—
Juvenile literature. 4. Cosmology—Juvenile literature. I. Title. II. Series.
QC16.H33B36 2005
530'.092—dc22

2004009193

ISBN-13: 978-0-7660-2281-2

Printed in the United States of America

10 9 8 7 6 5 4 3

To Our Readers:
We have done our best to make sure all Internet Addresses in this book were
active and appropriate when we went to press. However, the author and the
publisher have no control over and assume no liability for the material
available on those Internet sites or on other Web sites they may link to. Any
comments or suggestions can be sent by e-mail to comments@enslow.com or
to the address on the back cover.

Illustration Credits: AP/Wide World Photos, pp. 7, 41, 110, 111;
ArtToday.com, pp. 56, 74, 86; Campix <http://www.campix.co.uk>, pp.
20, 26, 44, 67; Corel Corporation, p. 100; Dover Publications, Inc., p.
10; Enslow Publishers, Inc., pp. 60, 61, 80; Intel, p. 108; Library of
Congress, pp. 13, 48, 52; NASA Goddard Space Flight Center (NASA-
GSFC), pp. 50, 89; National Archives, p. 22.

Cover Illustration: NASA Goddard Space Flight Center (NASA-GSFC)
(background); Campix <http://www.campix.co.uk> (inset).

Contents

A Lucky Man

STEPHEN HAWKING LEANED OVER TO TIE his shoes. At first he could not do it. His hands trembled. The bow would not come. The knot did not hold. Stephen became frustrated, but like everything in his life, he knew if he focused and worked hard enough, he would be able to do it. Concentrating on the task at hand, he finished tying his shoes.

It was New Year's Eve, of 1962. Stephen Hawking was not a child. He was a twenty-one-year-old graduate student pursuing a doctoral degree at Cambridge University. Already he had mastered scientific principles too complex for most people to understand. He was working toward an advanced degree at an age when most people have not finished college.

Despite his achievement, Stephen was struggling with his shoelaces. The trouble began in the spring. Six months later it was worse. It was his holiday break from school, and he should have been having a good time.

His parents, Frank and Isobel, were throwing a boisterous New Year's Eve party at their rambling London home. Many of Stephen's best friends were there. John McClenhan, who had shared Stephen's love for science, was there. So too was Michael Church, who had spent hours discussing the meaning of life with Stephen when the two were in their early teens.

Best of all, Jane Wilde was there. Before the party the two shared little more than a polite hello, but as 1962 became 1963, they really hit it off. Their conversation lasted for hours. Before the night was over, he had asked her out. Jane accepted. For a young man who was extremely shy around women, this was nearly

Stephen Hawking is recognized today as one of the greatest minds in the history of theoretical physics.

as great an achievement as graduating from Oxford. Everything seemed to be going his way. But when he went to pour a glass of wine, most of it splashed onto the tablecloth. A few of the guests probably thought Stephen was drunk.

Frank Hawking suspected something much more serious.

He was right.

Instead of enjoying the rest of his holiday, Stephen spent the new year enduring a series of painful tests.

"They took a muscle sample from my arm, stuck electrodes into me, and injected some radio-opaque fluid into my spine and watched it going up and down with X-rays as they tilted the bed," Stephen said, recalling his experiences in a hospital one bleak January day. The doctors would tell him little, and he "didn't feel like asking for more details, because they were obviously bad."[1]

The doctors were not sure what was wrong with him. His father, Frank, was a doctor himself. He was afraid Stephen had caught a virus during a summer trip to the Middle East.

When the diagnosis was finally made, it was much more serious than a virus. Stephen Hawking had Amyotrophic Lateral Sclerosis (ALS). In the United States, it is commonly called Lou Gehrig's disease.

Back on July 4, 1939, thirty-six-year-old Gehrig had stepped up to the microphone before a packed Yankee ballpark. During the break between a double-header, the team gave Gehrig an award. He had played more consecutive games than anyone else—fourteen years without missing a game. That April, he had suddenly retired.

As he began to speak, most in attendance already knew Gehrig was sick. They just did not realize how seriously.

"Fans, for the past two weeks you have been reading about a bad break," he told them that day. "Yet today I consider myself the luckiest man on the face of the earth."[2]

Two years later, Lou Geherig was dead.

ALS is commonly referred to as Lou Gehrig's disease in the United States. It was named for baseball great Lou Gehrig, who suffered from the disease.

In 1963, the prognosis for ALS sufferers was just as bleak. The disease was fatal. According to the doctors, Stephen would not live past twenty-five.

The doctors were wrong.

As Stephen Hawking's body grew weaker, his mind seemed to grow stronger. Confined first to crutches and then to a wheelchair, he imagined an expanding universe. He completed work that stumped Albert Einstein. He envisioned the beginning of the universe, even the beginning of time. He studied cosmology, which looks at how the universe began. At one time most scientists considered cosmology a pseudoscience—a false science. Stephen quickly brought it respect.

Thousands of years ago, what people believed about the universe mainly depended on where they were born. Science had little to do with it. Mythology, religion, observation—all blended into a belief system about the earth and its place in the nighttime sky.

People who lived in Babylon (where Iraq is today), would probably have seen the universe as an enormous mountain emerging from the sea. The sky rested inside an open dome (similar to the lip of an active volcano). Like an actor crossing a stage, the sun entered through one door and crossed the sky before exiting another.

Beliefs in ancient India were also based on myth. People there saw the earth as flat, supported on the back of a huge turtle. This turtle rested on another turtle, which rested on another, and so on—into infinity. Thousands of years ago, how giant turtles breathed in the airless universe was not a question they were able to ask.

Today these beliefs seem ridiculous, but they were as close as ancient people came to science.

Aristotle was one of the earliest cosmologists. Around 350 B.C., he combined the knowledge of sailors who relied on stars to guide their ships with the Babylonian idea of a stationary earth. Few of his ideas survived the test of time. Aristotle was important because he was one of the first people to apply scientific methods to what most considered part of religion.

The ancient philosopher and scientist Aristotle was one of the first to study cosmology.

Greek sailors had noticed how the planet's horizon seemed to curve away from them. Eratosthenes was the first to use mathematics to prove the world was not flat. Placing sticks in land near Aswan and Alexandria and recording observations of them at the same time of day, he noticed something interesting. The shadows did not match. When the sun was directly over Aswan at noon it did not cast a shadow, yet at the same time of day, a shadow formed beneath the stick at Alexandria. This suggested that the sun crossed the sky over a round planet. He used this information not only to calculate the Earth's shape, but also its size. His calculation was remarkably close to the true figure.

Pythagoras also applied mathematics to his study of the universe—calculating the distance between the earth and the sun. However, his figures were far less accurate. It was not his technique that was at fault. It was the technology.

It took many centuries before scientists could even begin to calculate the size and age of the universe. They used instruments such as radio telescopes as well as complicated mathematical equations. The greatest advances in cosmology began in the 1960s, just as Stephen Hawking was working on his doctoral thesis. As his disease slowly imprisoned his body, he was able to apply his mind to the work at hand. He could memorize complicated formulas others needed to write down. He worked the way he did because of ALS—it became harder and harder to type or hold a pen. In many ways this helped him find solutions where others failed.

Controversy

THE ROMAN INQUISITORS ARRESTED Galileo Galilei. They were a fearsome bunch. The elderly astronomer was charged with heresy: He had argued against an article of faith. If they found him guilty they could execute him. In the 1600s, that could mean being beheaded or even being tied to a stake and burned alive.

The Roman Inquisition was an offshoot of the better-known Spanish Inquisition that began in 1231. Operating under the power of the Catholic Church, the Inquisition could imprison, torture, or even kill anyone who defied their rule. Those who questioned the faith faced imprisonment. It did not matter if you were a bishop or a cardinal. It did not even matter if you were a respected author in your seventies, like Galileo.

Operating a telescope of his own design—one vastly improved over earlier, cruder versions—Galileo made a series of startling discoveries that are described in his book *Starry Messenger*. Some believe they changed the world more than any discoveries before or since.

However, it was his later work that would so upset the powers in Rome. He attempted to prove that the earth was not the center of the universe. (Polish scientist Nicolaus Copernicus had made such claims in a book that was published the same year he died, in 1543. Galileo agreed with the Copernican model of a sun-centered universe.) Galileo studied Jupiter, identifying its four moons, all of which revolve around the large planet. Examining Venus through his lens, he noticed a shadow cast by the sun.

Galileo's attempts to prove that everything in the heavens did not revolve around the earth contradicted seventeenth-century Catholic belief. The Church believed that God created the earth for man to dominate. The world was not only the center of God's love, it was the center of the universe.

In Italy during the 1600s, the only organization wealthy enough to fund education and scientific exploration was the Catholic Church. They educated young men in the sciences and in Latin, the language of both Catholic Mass and science. Although the Church produced numerous scholars, these researchers were expected to fit their discoveries into the narrow confines of religion.

Galileo did not just oppose the scientific beliefs of the time; he wrote a book about his discoveries, *Dialogue Concerning the Two Chief Systems of the World—Ptolemic and Copernican,* in accessible Italian. This work was widely read, and average citizens began buying or building crude telescopes, looking for proof in the night sky.

Not long after the book's publication, the Inquisition banned its sale, and Galileo was brought before the Inquisitors. Asked to recant his belief that the earth revolves around the sun, he reportedly replied, "E pur si muove" ("And it does move"). Sentenced to life imprisonment, Galileo actually endured a kind of house arrest. He spent most of his remaining years beneath the watchful eyes of armed guards in his home near Florence.

Exactly three hundred years after Galileo's death, on January 8, 1642, another scientific challenger was born. His ideas were just as controversial, but the man born on January 8, 1942 was not punished for them.

He was celebrated.

Stephen William Hawking was born in Oxford, England, to Frank and Isobel Hawking. As he later pointed out, "I estimate that about two hundred thousand other babies were also born on that day; I don't know whether any of them were later interested in astronomy."[1]

Stephen's mother arrived at the university town a few days before he was born and checked

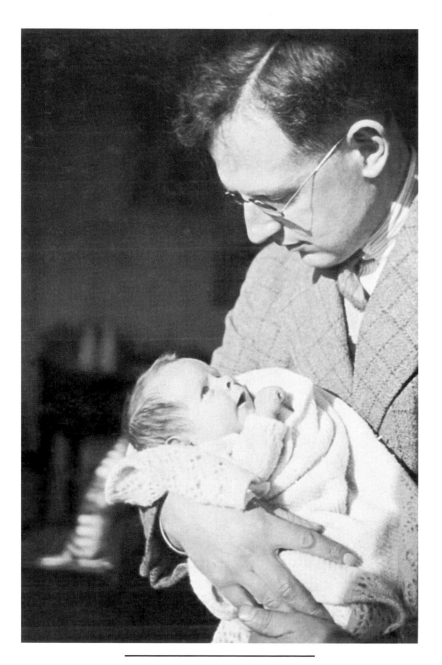

An infant Stephen Hawking is held by his father, Frank Hawking.

into a nearby hospital. A couple of weeks after Stephen was born, she returned to London.

Isobel lived in Oxford as a young woman, but that is not why she went there. By 1942, Oxford was one of the few safe places left in England. The Hawkings celebrated the arrival of their first child. Across Europe—and indeed much of the world—there was little cause for celebration.

Less than a decade before, a man who was a failed painter and imprisoned revolutionary was made the leader of Germany. His name was Adolph Hitler. Hitler's dark ambitions cost millions of people their lives.

Following the 1919 Versailles peace treaty ending World War I (then known as the Great War), Germany was forced to repay huge war debts. The cost of living skyrocketed. Average citizens could barely afford food and shelter. Adolph Hitler promised to return his country to greatness. Many believed him. Combining anti-Semitism (hatred of Jewish people) with dreams of world domination, he was appointed

Stephen Hawking was born in the midst of World War II, when England was threatened by the Nazi government of Germany, led by Adolph Hitler. Hitler had hoped to set his government up in Oxford following the war.

Chancellor of Germany by the country's president in 1933.

By 1942, Hitler's army was well on its way to making his dreams of conquest a reality. Already they had invaded Russia, France, Poland, and Holland. German troops were massed along the Russian border, and Germany had united with Italy and Japan. England was one of the few countries in Western Europe that Hitler hadn't defeated or established as an ally.

Some worried defeat was just a matter of time. But, just a month before Stephen's birth, on December 7, 1941, the Japanese mounted a sneak attack on Pearl Harbor. The United States was plunged into the war.

Stephen grew up in Highgate, a suburb of London. Night after night the city suffered the relentless bombing campaigns of the German air force. Once a home near the Hawking's was destroyed by a V-2 missile, a long range rocket launched from Germany. Their house lost a few windows, but fortunately the family was not home at the time.

During World War II, Oxford remained untouched. Home to one of the most respected universities in the world, Oxford boasted centuries-old buildings. It was also where Hitler hoped to headquarter his government after winning the war. "Oxford was a good place to be born during the war," Hawking later explained. "The Germans had an agreement that they would not bomb Oxford and Cambridge [another major university town], in return for the British not bombing Heidelberg and Gottingen. It is a pity that this civilized sort of arrangement couldn't have been extended to more areas."[2]

For Frank and Isobel Hawking, Oxford was more than peaceful. It was familiar. Both had received their educations there during the 1930s. At that time, attending college was rare for a woman. Despite Isobel's achievement, she was working as a secretary at a research institute when she met Frank. He had graduated from Oxford with a medical degree years before, focusing on tropical diseases.

Frank's career took him into the wilds of Africa. It was a dangerous, exciting job. Unlike the stereotypical gung-ho adventurer, he was a quiet, shy, and bookish man.

Opposites often attract, and outgoing Isobel was the perfect complement to the introspective Frank. The couple dated and married.

During World War II Frank tried to enlist. The British government did not want him in the Army. They needed him to continue his research. In most wars, disease kills more soldiers than bullets. Frank's efforts helped prevent needless deaths.

World War II ended with the German surrender on May 8, 1945, and the surrender of the Japanese on August 15th. By then Frank had risen to Head of the Division of Parisitology at the National Institute of Medical Research.

The job took him away from home. Stephen did not see his dad as much as he might have liked. Still, there was no question that Frank Hawking wanted the best for him. In England, attending the right private school was everything.

Stephen Hawking is pictured here at age twelve in the garden of his St. Albans home.

Private schools educated the elite men of England (few women were in powerful positions in the mid-twentieth century). These men ran everything from the government to corporations.

The grandson of a successful farmer who lost all he owned in World War I, and the son of a father barely able to afford tuition, Frank believed his second-rate early education had held him back. He wanted to give his son a better shot at success. In 1952, he selected Westminster Academy, a highly respected school that could do just that. Frank Hawking's salary would not cover tuition any more than his own father's had. Stephen needed a scholarship. Unfortunately, Stephen was too sick to take the entrance exam (his mother later wondered if the "glandular fever" doctors diagnosed might have been the first symptoms of ALS). Stephen Hawking's shot at Westminster disappeared.

Luckily for Stephen, his back-up school was almost as respected.

In 1950, his family had moved to St. Albans, a town twenty miles from Highgate. The Hawking home was in the shadows of a third-century cathedral that had once dominated the skyline and once dominated the life of the community. Built soon after St. Alban's founding in 303 A.D., the church symbolized the traditional values still dominating British society in the 1950s. Upper-middle-class and a bit stuffy, the town was the kind of place Stephen would soon want to leave.

But first, he went to school there. Stephen had been a student at the St. Albans School for Girls (which admitted boys until they turned ten) and he passed the exam admitting him to the all-boys high school. Although the school rejected two students for every one it let in, St. Albans School was not considered as "posh" or "upper class" as Westminster.

"I got an education there that was as good as, if not better than, I would have had at Westminster," Stephen recalled. "I have never found that my lack of social graces has been a hindrance."[3]

Attending St. Albans was not easy. Even as a pre-teen, Stephen was a bit odd. Concealing his scrawny body in rumpled clothes, he spoke quickly and with a slight lisp, so that his sentences were often a jumble of words that many people had a hard time understanding. Michael Church called it "Hawkingese," noting how Stephen had "a way of talking that collapsed words, sometimes quite creatively. I remember once he talked not about 'silhouettes' but about 'slit-outs,' which is actually quite an interesting collapse of the word."[4]

His entire family was considered eccentric. His father was away on work so often that Stephen's sister Mary later said, "I always had the impression that fathers were like migratory birds. They were there for Christmas, and then they vanished until the weather got warm. The fact that everybody else's father seemed to be around at this time of year just convinced me that other people's fathers were a bit odd."[5]

Stephen's mother tried to make up for her husband's absences. However, to his friends she probably seemed as weird as her son. In the conservative 1950s, Isobel was ahead of her time.

Wearing homemade clothes and participating in protests and labor strikes, she would have been called a "hippie" ten years later. She even joined the Communist Party.

Inside their house, furniture bled stuffing onto the floors while the wallpaper displayed so many stains and tears it looked like a bad abstract painting. Rarely concerned with appearances, the family traveled in a used taxi. Once they drove all the way to India in their new Ford Consul automobile. It was one of the few excursions Stephen missed.

His bedroom could barely contain the hodge-podge of textbooks, test tubes, and his never-ending experiments. His friends were all bright, but they did not always get good grades. Stephen was far from the top of his class, but as he explained to his mother, there were quite a few smart kids attending St. Albans.

Homework may have suffered, but his friends devoured complicated books or concentrated on advanced science and math. The small cluster of friends had endless discussions about everything from politics to chemistry, subjects they would not study in school for years.

Instead of playing games made by other people, Stephen designed his own. Based on combat or kings and queens, the rules were almost impossible to follow. His sister Mary recalled that "he ended up with a fearful game called Dynasty, which, as far as I can make out . . . went on forever because there was no way of ending it."[6]

Coming up with complex ideas few understood would soon become familiar. Explaining ideas to those who could not easily grasp them was excellent training for the future science writer. Inside his cluttered bedroom, he guided his friends through these imaginary worlds and negotiated their heated arguments over the outcome of games he had designed.

When they were not discussing games, they were discussing religion. His friends Graham Dow and Roger Ferneyhaugh were inspired by preacher Billy Graham's sermons and became "born-again Christians." Others in the group became fascinated by extra-sensory perception (ESP), how the mind operates beyond the five senses of sight, sound, smell, taste, and touch. Evidence of the existence of ESP is highly debatable, but many believers think it is possible to move objects just by concentrating, or to read minds.

Stephen examined his friends' beliefs and found them wanting. He did not accept the evidence for ESP. Whenever Stephen concluded that an idea lacked proof, he did not just consider it silly—he considered its believers pretty silly as well.

Once, Michael Church went on and on about a mystical subject while Stephen quietly listened. All at once Michael realized, "he was encouraging me to make a fool of myself, and watching me as though from a great height. It was a profoundly unnerving moment."[7]

Although he liked his friends, Stephen felt like an outsider. He was someone with a doubting attitude. The board games trained him to think about complex ideas, and his skeptical attitude taught him to question. Good training for a scientist but controversial for a friend. Few people like it when they realize they are not being taken seriously.

Stephen had little time for ESP, because there were too many advances being made in "real" science. He lingered over mathematical formulas with their precise outcomes. By the time he was fourteen, his talents for problem solving set him ahead of his classmates.

More significant, Stephen began applying what he learned. As a sophomore, he constructed a crude computer. Far from the complex PCs built today, Stephen's construction was little more than a huge calculator. Still, it did more than just add numbers; it also gave Stephen his first taste of fame.

"The machine answers some useless, though quite complex, logical problems. Last term's meetings of the society were devoted to it and proved lively and well attended," his school paper the *Albanian* reported.[8]

Despite the praise, Stephen was facing a

challenge at home. His father had already mapped out a career path for his son—one devoted to medicine, not math. Frank Hawking wanted Stephen to become a doctor. In order to pursue his dreams, Stephen needed to do more than get into a good mathematics program at a university. He needed to convince his father to let him go.

A Lazy Student?

AFTER KING HENRY II FORBADE BRITISH college students to travel to Paris, they were forced to attend more local schools. It was 1167 A.D. and enrollment at Oxford University immediately swelled. Although nearly a century old, it grew rapidly after the King's decision. With every passing century, Oxford's reputation grew as well.

Life at the university was more than just academic. During the Middle Ages it could be dangerous. In the 1200s, after riots between students and townspeople, residence halls were built. A few centuries later, on October 16, 1555, the Bishop of Worcester, Hugh Latimer, and student Nicholas Ridley were burned at the stake in Oxford; the Archbishop of Canterbury, Thomas Cranmer followed them in flames the next year.

By the time Stephen Hawking toured the campus, it was the oldest English speaking university in the world. The very walls seemed to echo with the voices of nearly a thousand years of education.

In 1959, Stephen was thinking quite a bit about history and tradition. Not Oxford's history but his father's, and not the tradition of the school he was applying to but the tradition Frank Hawking wanted to begin.

Frank was convinced a math major would have a tough time earning a living. He wanted his son to major in biology and prepare for medical school. Stephen was not interested. Already his mind was focused on larger things— the entire universe. He wanted to study physics, which is the branch of science that looks at matter and energy and how the two interact.

Despite Stephen's objections to his father's

plans, he agreed to one condition. He enrolled at his father's old college.

Oxford University is composed of over thirty separate colleges, including the University College his father graduated from. As soon as Stephen agreed, his father set up a meeting with the man who would be Stephen's physics tutor if he were accepted. Robert Berman would help decide whether or not Stephen was admitted. Frank Hawking hoped the meeting would help his son get in.

The meeting was unnecessary.

"When I first met Stephen, he was probably still not seventeen . . . his father did most of the talking; I didn't really get much impression of Stephen," Berman recalled. "But when he took the entrance exam, he did very well, especially in the physics."[1]

As Berman remembered, after Stephen met with the senior members of the faculty, they all agreed not only to let him enter as a physics major, but to give him a scholarship as well.

In the fall of 1959, Stephen began attending

University College at Oxford University. In the beginning little was different from high school. He still did not study very hard. Often Stephen would go over a large set of math problems the day it was due. His peers would struggle to finish three or four; he would do a dozen right before class. It was almost too easy. He got good grades and won awards, "He was obviously the brightest student I've ever had," Berman later pointed out.[2]

Good grades were not enough. Stephen was bored. He had felt like an outsider his entire life and Oxford was not any different. His first year was even lonelier than high school. He could not make any new friends and most of his old ones were at other schools.

When he returned to Oxford for his second year, he set about improving his social life with an energy he rarely devoted to homework. Stephen joined the crew team.

Rowing, or crew, was a popular sport at Oxford. Teams consisted of seven rowers and a coxswain who shouted commands and motivated them from the ship's bow. It required hard work and dedication. Rowers arose early every morning, even on the weekends. They rowed in the freezing cold and the blistering sun, in rain and fog.

Sometimes they sliced through the thin ice crusting over the Thames.

Each year the crews held recruiting parties.

Stephen was all for it.

Writer David Filkin remembers meeting Stephen. "Eight of the . . . rugby team, including myself, stood uneasily on board the beautiful old college barge, waiting to try our hands at rowing for the first time. . . It soon dawned on me that we were not alone. A much smaller figure stood alongside our group, distinguished by a blazer instead of a rugby shirt, huge dark horn rimmed spectacles, and an immaculate straw boater."[3]

The boater—a distinctive straw hat—was not the only thing different about Stephen. His size made him an unlikely jock. Crew members needed to be muscular and athletic. Except for the coxswain. As the one member who did not row, being small was an advantage. In his position, Stephen put as much energy into winning as the rowers did.

In competition, boats lined up one behind the other. Where it passes though Oxford, the Thames is too narrow for boats to race abreast of each other like sprinters on a land race. Instead, in order to pass, each boat had to bump the boat in front. The bumped boat would pull over to the side. Over the course of several days, a boat in the rear could move up several places— the boat that moved up the most could win.

As rugby players, the members of Stephen's team were ill-suited for the competition. They had the strength but lacked endurance. After the boat behind them was bumped out of the race, the challenge only grew. Now they'd never be able to relax.

They did not give up. Under Stephen's shouted commands, the team rowed relentlessly. They did not win, but everyone on the team realized they would never have done as well without him as coxswain.

Crew gave Stephen access to a social life he

had not enjoyed freshman year. There were parties and pubs, jokes and loud stories. It was everything college life was supposed to be. And when his required lab time meant he would not be able to crew enough, he cut down on the lab time. Crew was suddenly more important than his work in school.

"The prevailing attitude at Oxford at that time was very antiwork," Stephen recalled in his book *Black Holes and Baby Universes*. "You were

In order to make friends and feel accepted Stephen joined the crew team at Oxford. His small size made him suitable to be the coxswain on the team.

supposed to be brilliant without effort, or to accept your limitations and get a fourth-class degree ... the physics course at Oxford was arranged in a way that made it particularly easy to avoid work. I did one exam before I went up, then had three years at Oxford with just the final exams at the end."[4]

Stephen figures he spent *maybe* an hour a day studying during his time in college. His lax study habits caught up with him. During his final semester, he realized how completely unprepared he was for the upcoming exams. He had coasted, relying on his intuition more than anything he learned. At Oxford, the regular grades and exams most college students in the United States dread do not exist. It was shocking for Stephen to realize how poorly prepared he was for the tests that would determine his future.

It was not a question of whether or not he would go to graduate school. It was a question of where. After considering his options, Stephen realized he wanted to focus on cosmology. Although Oxford did not have a professor he could study with, Cambridge did—Fred Hoyle, a man Stephen later described as "the most distinguished British astronomer of the time."[5]

If he got into Cambridge, he could work towards a Ph.D. studying under Hoyle. If he stayed at Oxford, he did not know what he would do.

Because of Hoyle's reputation, admission to the cosmology program was very competitive. Stephen needed to graduate with a first-class degree.

Stephen studied as he had never studied before. In his favor, he would be graded only on the questions he answered. He could ignore any he did not understand. It was then that he decided to focus on theoretical physics instead of scientific questions based on fact. If he stuck to theory, he knew his intuition would help him out. The decision was made in haste, but focusing on a branch of physics where the science took place more in one's imagination than in laboratory experiments would deeply affect the rest of his life. He could not have

Stephen Hawking is pictured here at his Oxford graduation.

known it then, but if he had focused on a more "hands on" branch of science he never could have succeeded.

The night before his test, he could not sleep. For the first time he worried about a physics test. The next day, exhausted, Stephen did not do as well as he needed to. His grades put him on the line between a first- and second-class degree. So, Stephen met with faculty members and was interviewed.

One of them asked Stephen what he would do after graduation. He looked at his questioner and replied that if he received a first he would go to Cambridge, but if he wound up with a second, he had to stay at Oxford. Maybe they wanted to see him succeed, or maybe they were tired of him. Regardless, they gave him a first. The entire universe awaited.

4

Cosmic Eggs and Big Bangs

THREE CENTURIES BEFORE STEPHEN Hawking was accepted at Cambridge University, the school was closed when the bubonic plague swept across Europe. In the Middle Ages the plague devastated the continent, killing one out every four people there. It reappeared in the 17th century. Nearly 70,000 people died in London during The Great Plague of 1665–1666 (again about one-quarter of the population). Yet for one young college graduate, the disease altered life in a surprisingly positive way.

Isaac Newton had just received a bachelors degree from Cambridge in 1665 when the plague shut down the campus. Newton went back to his birthplace, Woolsthorpe, England. The disease forced him to abandon his postgraduate plans; otherwise he would have stayed at school, following the lessons of older instructors. On his own, Newton's discoveries were unhindered by their beliefs.

"All this was in the two plague years of 1665 and 1666," he later wrote to the Huguenot scholar Pierre Des Maizeaux. "For in those days I was in my prime of my age of invention & minded Mathematics and Philosophy more than at any time since."[1]

Over the next year and a half his discoveries were so amazing that they have stood the test of time. They created a foundation for modern physics and cosmology. These two fields would intersect almost exactly three hundred years later.

The last twelve months of Newton's work would later be called his "miracle year." He believed that what he was learning could be applied throughout the world, even the universe, so he did not call them theories. He called them laws.

Many of Newton's laws dealt with gravity, the invisible force affecting objects and the ways they interact. He looked at the effect of gravity on the sun and the planets (the solar system). Although

Sir Isaac Newton made many discoveries that would later serve as the building blocks of physics and cosmology.

he crafted the law of gravity from observation, the story of him discovering it after being bonked on the head by an apple is questionable. Other laws he formed through experiments and complicated mathematical formulae. One law describes how an object changes its motion when sufficient force is applied. It was so precise that three hundred years later The National Aeronautics and Space Administration (NASA) relied upon it to launch the space shuttle.

When Stephen Hawking entered Cambridge, he did not expect to have his own miracle year. Although his work would not be as earth shattering as Newton's, it was tremendously important.

After all, what's more important than discovering the beginning of the universe?

When Hawking arrived at Cambridge, he received some disappointing news. The man he had come to study with, Sir Fred Hoyle, was not available. He had been one of the main reasons Hawking had applied in the first place. Still, just beginning his doctoral work in

Newton's laws of gravity are applied today in preparing space shuttle launches.

cosmology was a relief. Like many of his peers in their early twenties, Hawking's dreams were coming into focus. He had known that he did not want to get his doctorate examining sunspots at Oxford. He knew he preferred cosmology to other branches of astronomy.

In order to earn his Ph.D., Hawking needed to write a doctoral thesis, a complicated paper demonstrating his qualifications for the degree. Hawking called his thesis, "Properties of an Expanding Universe." Although Hawking's cosmological hero was Galileo, much of his work was based on the re-examination of Newton's laws that began in the early twentieth century.

Despite numerous challenges, these laws had proven accurate for hundreds of years—with one exception. In 1905, Albert Einstein disproved Newton's law of absolute time and space. The papers that Einstein wrote that year radically altered twentieth-century physics.

The speed of light travels at a fixed speed of 186,281 miles per second. Einstein believed that if the speed of light did not change, then

Albert Einstein was considered a genius and made many important advances in the field of physics.

something else must. That something is time. If someone could travel inside a spaceship moving near light speed, time would be affected. Such high-speed space travel was like an "anti-aging device." The traveler might believe just a year had passed, but when she returned to earth, her friends could have aged twenty years.

At the time, Einstein was unknown in the scientific community and his theories were so radical that few paid any attention, let alone challenged him. Yet over the next decade, Einstein's theories, including his re-examination of part of Newton's law of gravity, began to earn him notice. Einstein believed gravity is not responsible for the earth's movement through space. Instead space itself is responsible.

Newton's law assumed that the sun exerted its gravitational pull on the earth. Einstein imagined a situation where the sun simply disappeared. It would still take eight minutes for light from the sun to reach the earth. Yet a careful reading of Newton's law indicated that the gravitational change from a missing sun would be felt instantly. The law seemed to claim gravitational forces could move faster than the speed of light. Accepting that nothing can do that immediately discredited Newton's law.

Using a complicated mathematical formula (that relies on twenty simultaneous equations with ten unknown quantities), Einstein demonstrated the relationship between the curvature of space and the distribution of mass in the universe. He showed that it was curved space itself, not gravity, that affects the movements of objects like the earth and the sun.

This theory would have enormous implications—implications that affected the work of Hawking over half a century later.

But in the early 1900s, the problem with Albert Einstein's theories was that so few people understood them. In 1919, astronomy professor Arthur Eddington was asked if he was truly one of only three people on the planet who did. It took him a moment to answer and the question was repeated. "I am trying to think who the third person is," he reportedly replied.[2]

It took a fortuitous solar eclipse to prove Einstein's theories and give them wider respect. If his concept of curved space was true, then during an eclipse, starlight passing at the periphery of the sun would appear to be slightly displaced (moved).

On May 29, 1919, Eddington observed an eclipse from the island of Principe, on the coast of Africa. Using photographic plates, Eddington was able to demonstrate that starlight was displaced exactly as Einstein had predicted.

Although Einstein's theories gained wider respect, they were also re-examined, just as he had done with Newton's laws. Despite the complicated formulas he used, Einstein was no mathematician. The "unknown quantities" he relied upon would be repeatedly questioned.

German mathematician Karl Schwarzschild was one of the first to produce an exact solution, instead of just an approximate one. The work he did would someday be re-created with a computer. Schwarzschild used paper and pencil.

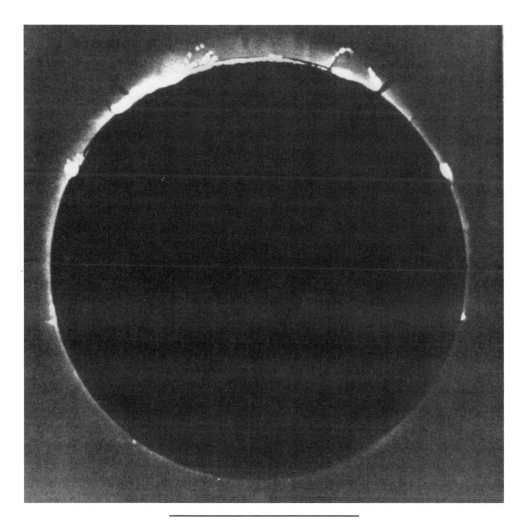

An image of a solar eclipse.

He showed how space curves around an object based upon its distance from the object's center.

This seems simple enough, but the most troubling aspect of the mathematician's work was generally ignored. He calculated that there is a critical point at which curvature is so strong, matter cannot escape. This curve is called the Schwazschild Radius. When the force of curved space is sufficient, matter continues to compress, growing smaller and smaller. Exerted upon the earth, it would quickly reduce our planet to the size of a lima bean. The same force would compress our sun to an object just a few miles across. The compressed matter would be very dense; a tablespoon could weigh a ton!

Applying the Schwarzschild Radius to stars makes sense. Stars radiate heat and maintain their enormous size through explosion. When fuel runs out, objects are subjected to enormous pressure because of space curvature. But an object many times the size of our sun would end up more than just a dense object. It would become a singularity—a single point in the center.

The Schwarzschild Radius would be very significant to Hawking, as would the work of Alexander Friedmann. In 1922, Friedman had corrected an error in one of Einstein's computations and showed that the universe was indeed expanding.

A few years later, Belgian cosmologist Abbe Georges LeMaitre used Friedmann's equations to postulate the beginning of the universe. He called it "the cosmic egg."

The "cosmic egg" does not just represent the beginning of the universe. It represents the beginning of space. Under this theory, the beginning is *not* a firecracker exploding into a darkened room, showering sparks of light like stars across the floor. Instead, Lemaitre believed the beginning of the universe was like a cosmic egg, with every ingredient necessary to form everything in the universe packed tightly inside, *including space.*

The cosmic egg theory fascinated Hawking. It was so hard to picture the idea that before the universe began what we think of as space did not exist. Everything was tucked inside that cosmic egg.

As he began work on his doctorate, studying the expanding universe, he could not help but notice the theories of the man he had thought would be teaching him. Along with Hermann Bondi and Thomas Gold, Fred Hoyle was a supporter of the steady state theory of the universe. This theory suggests that matter is continuously being created as the universe expands slowly and consistently, with no beginning or end, just a series of events.

Hoyle even named the opposing theory. During a radio talk show in England he said that the idea that the universe was created in a single explosion from the cosmic egg was "ridiculous, I call it the big bang."[3]

The name stuck.

In 1962, the big bang theory had few supporters. Stephen Hawking was about to become one of them.

His research was not going anywhere. He was bored with his studies, bored with life. At

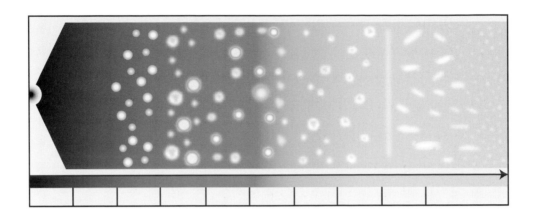

This diagram of the Big Bang shows how everything in the universe came from one small point or cosmic egg.

Cambridge, doctoral students were given a great deal of freedom. In fact, they were encouraged to interact with the other students. Hawking began helping Jayant Narlikar. Narlikar was performing calculations supporting Hoyle's steady state theory.

Without Hoyle's knowledge, Stephen began adding the figures himself. The work was more interesting than his project. And by early 1963, Hawking needed all the diversions he could find. During his winter break, Hawking had been diagnosed with ALS.

"[S]hortly after I came out of [the] hospital,

I dreamed that I was going to be executed," he recalled. "I suddenly realized that there were a lot of worthwhile things I could do if I were reprieved. One result of my illness: when one is faced with the possibility of an early death, it makes one realize that life is worth living."[4]

Hawking did not immediately return to his own work. Instead, he kept going over Narlikar's equations. What he discovered would change his life as surely as ALS had.

Hoyle began discussing his research at The Royal Society of London. Over one-hundred people attended, but some of them wondered if

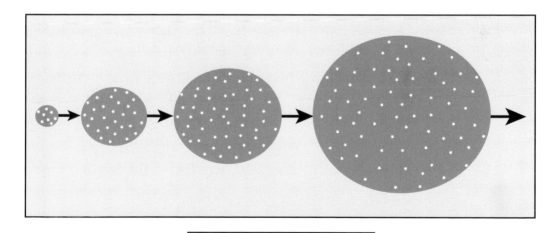

People opposed to the big bang theory felt the universe was constantly expanding, also known as the steady state theory.

he was ready. Usually before research is presented, other scientists review it. No one had seen Hoyle's work except for the man himself and his research assistant.

Hoyle did not know about Hawking.

However, Hoyle was very well known, and the usual requirements were waived. When he concluded his speech, the crowd applauded boisterously, except for one man.

Hoyle asked if there were any questions.

Stephen Hawking rose awkwardly, relying on a walking stick for balance. In a quiet, clear voice he said, "The quantity you're talking about diverges."

Quite simply, the numbers did not add up. The audience began whispering back and forth. Could what this young man said be true? If it was, then Hoyle's entire discussion was pointless. If the numbers did not add up, he had not proved his theory.

"Of course it doesn't diverge," Hoyle angrily replied.

"It does." Hawking was sure of himself. He knew he was right.

"How do you know?"

"Because I worked it out."[5]

Hoyle did not realize that the young graduate student had spent more time with the older cosmologist's theory than with his own thesis. That day Hawking earned a name for himself even as the debate between big bang and steady state believers grew fiercer.

5

The Beginning of Time

NOT VERY LONG AGO, IT SEEMED LIKE the only people interested in cosmology were retired scientists with too much time on their hands and science-fiction dreamers preparing their next novel. It did not get much respect. Few young graduate students considered a career in it.

Beginning in the late 1950s and early 1960s that began to change. One reason was that astronomers were able to make observations proving the cosmologists' theories. Just as important was the groundbreaking work of a few young dedicated cosmologists like Stephen Hawking.

After he proved that the numbers used in Fred Hoyle's steady state theory did not add up, Hawking gained respect. Hoyle practically *was* the Cambridge cosmology program. His reputation was diminished, even as Hawking's grew. Hoyle claimed that it was unethical for someone to double-check his figures without his permission, but many fellow scientists wondered why he had publicly presented a paper without the necessary checking.

Because of the controversy, Hawking's name became widely known among scientists. Unfortunately, although they knew who Stephen Hawking was, he had earned his reputation disproving someone else's work.

Hawking had work of his own to do.

Before the Cambridge Ph.D. program, he had never devoted much energy to anything. Worse, most people assumed he would be dead before he could earn a doctorate. His father was certain time was running out. Fred Hawking begged Stephen's advisor, Dennis Sciama, to speed his son along. Sciama refused. The Ph.D.

program took a prescribed amount of time to finish. Nothing could change that—not Fred Hawking's pleas, nor Stephen's deteriorating condition.

After his diagnosis, Hawking struggled with depression, listening to dark compositions by Richard Wagner. As his mother explained, "Stephen was very badly depressed and he wasn't really very much inclined to go on with work, having been told he only had two and a half years. But meeting Jane really put him on his mettle. And he started to work."[1]

Following his confrontation with Hoyle, Hawking returned to campus re-energized. Still, it almost did not matter how much time Hawking had left, nor if the course was condensed. His thesis research hit a dead end. He did not know what to write about.

It took someone not even part of the Cambridge program to help Hawking find his way. Roger Penrose was a mathematician in his early thirties enjoying his own growing reputation. Penrose was re-examining the notion

Stephen Hawking and his first wife, Jane.

of singularity in collapsing stars. Although Karl Schwarzschild's 1915 work produced a mathematical singularity, scientists did not consider it a real singularity. This is because by simply changing one of the mathematical coordinates, the singularity was eliminated.

It was during a conversation at a Cambridge coffee shop with Sciama that Penrose wondered if he could apply his own mathematical techniques to the question of collapsing stars. When he did this, Penrose discovered a "real" singularity. During a London lecture, the mathematician told the audience he had proven that a singularity exists when a star collapses to a certain point. Afterwards, the star could never re-expand.

Students from the Department of Applied Mathematics and Theoretical Physics (DAMTP), including Hawking, had taken the train to Penrose's lecture. On the way back, inside the second-class compartment, Hawking zoned out. The conversation of the other cosmology students became a hum as he turned the ideas Penrose discussed around in his mind.

It was a "eureka" moment, the second when a scientist realizes [he has] found the solution to a troubling problem.

Hawking did not even wait for a pause in the chatter, but turned to Sciama who was sitting next to him and said, "I wonder what would happen if you applied Roger's singularity theory to the entire Universe."[2]

Albert Einstein's special theory of relativity, which he wrote in 1905, discusses how light travels at a constant speed and other motion is relative. Once it was proven, it became a cornerstone of many young physic students' education. In contrast, by the time Hawking had his insight, Einstein's 1916 theory of general relativity, which explains the effect of gravity on large objects, was rarely discussed.

By combining the theory of general relativity with complex math techniques pioneered by Penrose, Hawking realized something. The singularity for a collapsing star could be run in reverse—all the way to the beginning of the universe.

All the way back to the cosmic egg.

There was one problem. Hawking had just a year left to complete his work—he had spent the last two years on other matters when he should have been focusing on his Ph.D.

"I began to understand general relativity and made progress with my work," Hawking later said, "but what really made a difference was that I got engaged to a woman named Jane Wilde. This gave me something to live for, but it also meant that I had to get a job if we were to get married."[3]

He needed a job and he needed a Ph.D. As he dug into his thesis, he realized he enjoyed the labor. It did not really feel like work to him—as Hawking later pointed out, scientists are among the few people paid to do something they love.

He did more than take apart the steady state theory Hoyle championed. This theory held that the universe continues to expand and contract regularly, that there is no "beginning," no "end." Hawking's doctoral thesis presented mathematical proof that if one went backwards in time to the universe's beginnings, one would find a singularity. This is a point of infinite density and zero volume, a point containing all of the matter in the universe in a space too small to imagine. From this singularity the universe began with a "big bang."

Sciama was still a steady state proponent, but was impressed with Hawking's work. In fact, he even brought in Penrose to go over it. Penrose and Sciama agreed on one thing: Hawking's equations did not diverge. They added up.

The work Hawking did earned him a Ph.D. in 1965. Stephen Hawking became Dr. Stephen Hawking. He had decided to stay at Cambridge. The university enjoyed a worldwide reputation for cosmology, and it was familiar. Walking was becoming increasingly difficult for Hawking. He was not prepared to deal with a new campus.

Prior to his Ph.D., he had earned a fellowship in theoretical physics at Caius, another college within Cambridge. The job was low paying but allowed him to continue his research. He also became a professor, joining the graduate staff at the Institute for Theoretical Astronomy and becoming a teacher at the Department of Applied Mathematics and Theoretical Physics (DAMTP), a separate department established in the early 1960s by the head of the physics department at Cambridge, George Batchelor. Hawking's timing was excellent—the department was already earning a reputation for developing bold new theories in cosmology.

For someone who had shunned work before his illness, Hawking began working very hard indeed. He believed he had a death sentence hanging over his head. How he spent every day was important.

6

The Big and the Small of It

NINETEEN SIXTY-FIVE WAS A BIG YEAR for Hawking and a big year for cosmology. Besides earning his doctorate, he also got married. In July, he and Jane Wilde were wed in the chapel at Trinity Hall. She had been a great source of motivation and continued to encourage him to pursue his theories even when disease and controversy might have discouraged him.

By the time Hawking was awarded his doctorate, observational astronomy had moved beyond what could be seen. For centuries, the science meant looking at stars and other heavenly bodies through a telescope. As lenses improved, astronomers were able to see more and more, but their eyes limited them.

The reason scientists avoided examining the beginning of the universe until the early twentieth century was not lack of curiosity but limited technology. Studying the beginning of the universe meant looking across the vast reaches of distant galaxies, peering millions of years into the past (because starlight travels at a fixed speed from the star to the observer).

Advances in technology changed everything.

Scientists knew there was more to studying galaxies than what meets the eyes. Light moves

Advances in technology, such as better lenses in telescopes, have made it easier to explore the galaxies.

in waves along what is known as the "visible spectrum." In other words, light is visible to the naked eye, and magnifying tools such as telescopes simply improve one's ability to see it.

But the "invisible" spectrum is just as valuable. Light is only one part of the electromagnetic spectrum. By the late 1950s, almost all of the other portions could be observed. Devices were created to capture light from the ultraviolet and the infrared spectrums, as well as X-Rays, microwaves, and even gamma rays.

Still, it was with a traditional optical telescope in the Palomar Observatory that scientists discovered the faint smudge of a radio-emitting galaxy. Examining this galaxy's "signal," they determined that it rested one billion light years away (all members of the electromagnetic spectrum travel at light speed).

"The curtain was drawn back on the universe; we now had a much deeper look into space," noted Nobel Prize winning physicist Antony Hewish. "It turned out that as you looked back in time there were far more of these radio galaxies than would fit the steady state theory."[1]

The steady state theory saw the universe in a kind of balance, with galaxies being born and decaying. The big bang theory viewed the universe as constantly expanding from a central explosive point. Steady state believed the universe was pretty much the same one billion years ago as it would be one billion years from now. Improvements in radio telescopes allowed astronomers to look deep into the past—into a world that existed over one billion years ago.

This is possible because light (and other waves, such as microwaves) travels 186,000 miles per second, or 5,865,696,000,000 miles in a year. Although this seems like an enormous distance, stretched across the vast reaches of the universe it is not. Even the closest star is over four light years away. Looking at a star one billion light years away means seeing it as it was, not as it is. It could have died long ago.

The past *was* different. The universe was changing.

Big bang believers also thought the universe would always retain a few degrees of the heat generated after that first explosion. Just as a stove stays warm long after it is turned off, the universe should not have cooled off completely.

The temperature when substances no longer possess thermal energy—they do not give off any heat at all—is called absolute zero. This is a temperature of 459 degrees Fahrenheit. If the universe were measured at just a few degrees above this, it would provide further support for the big bang.

George Gamow predicted that the universe was "filled with a cosmic background radiation composed of ancient photons released by the big bang . . . the temperature of this radiation should be about five degrees above absolute zero."[2]

Scientists began looking for this temperature. Further study revealed that the peak radiation could be found in the microwave region of the electromagnetic spectrum.

The same year that Stephen and Jane

married, Princeton University's Robert Dicke was overseeing the construction of a microwave background detector. This device, Dicke believed, would uncover the radiation proving the big bang. The device was almost operational when the phone rang.

Half an hour away, a pair of researchers at Bell Laboratories had a problem. As Arno Penzias explained to Dicke, he and his partner Robert Wilson were struggling to eliminate radio interference on one of their antennae. Designed for satellite communications, the antennae had been transformed into a crude radio telescope. The device kept picking up a microwave radiation signal with a temperature less than three degrees above absolute zero. At first they had suspected pigeon droppings of interfering with the transmission. However, after climbing onto the roof and cleaning the antenna, the trouble remained. Could Dicke help them?

The Princeton professor rushed over to the lab, but even before he got there he was pretty sure he had been scooped. When he arrived at the lab, he quickly confirmed it. Penzias and Wilson had discovered the background radiation Gamow predicted. The pair would win the Nobel Prize for their work.

"The discovery of the microwave background in 1965 ruled out steady state theory," Hawking later said in an interview, "and showed that the universe must have been very hot and dense in the past."[3]

As Hawking's awareness of the universe expanded, his own world seemed to contract. Jane and Stephen moved into an apartment owned by the University. Located at 5 West Road, the spacious ground floor dwelling offered big rooms and wide doors. Soon he would need both: By the end of the decade Hawking had to move off his crutches and into a wheelchair. It was a painful step for him, a concession that he was not as independent as he would like to be. At least he was still alive. He had already beaten the odds the doctors gave him.

His doctoral thesis and papers he had written as a professor began earning Hawking international recognition. Teamed with Penrose, his acclaim increased. The two young scientists made their name with their theory of the beginning of the universe. Now they examined "the big crunch," the name given to its end. Hawking and Penrose believed that gravity

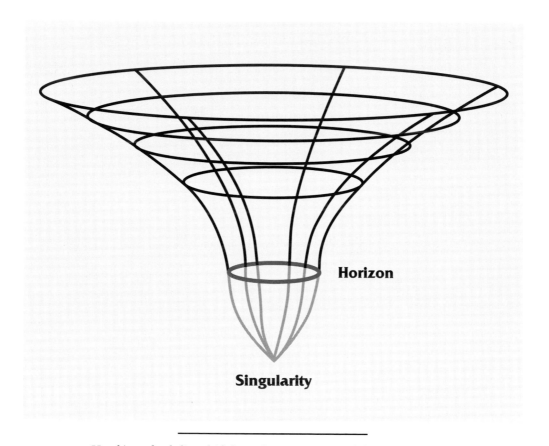

Horizon

Singularity

Hawking also believed if the universe was created from a cosmic egg then it will eventually collapse back into a point of singularity as illustrated in this diagram.

overcomes the universe's expansion (generated by that initial big bang explosion) and the galaxics would reach a boundary and then slowly begin moving backwards. Eventually, the entire universe would collapse, returning to a singularity. Working out the equations necessary for the big crunch theory, Hawking became the first scientist to combine the physics of the very small with the very large.

He had used Einstein's theory of general relativity when he was examining enormous bodies such as our sun and the stars. Looking at the beginning meant imagining the universe as an object even smaller than an atom. Hawking realized that a different branch of physics now came into play.

Quantum mechanics looks at the behavior of very small objects, such as atoms and photons. Hawking combined quantum mechanics and general relativity, something no other scientist had done.

Colleagues began to refer to Hawking as his generation's Einstein. Graduate students whispered his name like awed teenagers in the presence of the latest pop star.

In 1969, a scientist from New Jersey inspired Hawking. This time, it was Princeton University physics professor John Wheeler giving a speech in New York City. That speech would take a branch of science once belonging exclusively to retired scientists, fiction writers, and crackpots and offer it to the world.

Wheeler was tired of using the phrase "gravitationally collapsed stars." He decided to call them black holes. Two simple words, but words so descriptive that they begged to be included in newspaper and magazine articles. Soon the attention given to black holes would make Hawking more than an academic star. He would be a media celebrity as well.

Black Holes and White Dwarfs

IT IS TOUGH TO IMAGINE TWO WORDS IN science sparking the imaginations of more writers and filmmakers than "black hole." From the time they were first used by John Wheeler in 1969, television shows such as *Star Trek* and movies such as *Event Horizon* examined what would happen to someone pulled into one of these cosmic whirlpools.

Although some of the stories were based on science, most of them were wildly unrealistic. That is because understanding black holes means first understanding stars. Many of the wilder storytellers should have listened to Stephen Hawking's explanation:

> *Stars are formed when the mutual gravitational attraction between molecules floating in space, mostly hydrogen gas, causes lumps to form. [The molecules pull together and] gravity presses the molecules closer and closer together until they interact under high pressure causing an increase in temperature.*
>
> *As the gas glows it produces radiation of various wavelengths and as the compression increases, the interaction intensifies until the radiation is great enough to stop further the gravitational attraction.*[1]

A star is born.

Throughout the twentieth century, many scientists added to our understanding of stars. A paper written by Sir Arthur Eddington called "On the Internal Constitution of Stars" explained how a star "can be fueled by a reaction at its core providing the energy to heat continually the gas atoms."[2] Physicist Han Bethe proved that nuclear fusion kept a star burning bright. The first atomic bombs relied on nuclear *fission*—the action of the nucleus being violently split apart. Nuclear fusion, on the other hand, occurs when the nuclei of atoms combine to form larger nuclei, releasing enormous amounts of energy in the process. Nuclear fusion would later be applied to an even deadlier weapon, the hydrogen bomb.

Albert Einstein's most famous equation, $E=MC^2$, revealed exactly how much energy was produced as the star's mass was converted into heat and radiation, gradually burning its fuel.

So what happens when a star runs through its fuel? Well, as exciting as a star's birth may be, nothing is as spectacular as its death. "When a star burns up all its fuel, it collapses due to its own gravity," Hawking points out.[3]

How far it collapses depends on the star's size. The bigger it is, the further it collapses. Anything below one and one-half times the size of our sun collapses down to a white dwarf, a small star tinier than earth where just a teaspoon of material weighs hundreds of pounds.

Neutron stars are even denser. Resulting from the collapse of a star from one and one-half

Sometimes when stars collapse they become white dwarfs, as seen above.

to three times the size of our sun, they are about the size of a large city. A teaspoon of material taken from a neutron star would weigh millions of tons!

Only the most massive stars, objects over three times the size of our own sun, become black holes when they collapse. The challenge was finding a black hole in the darkness of space. Fortunately, the man who named them also explained how to locate one. Black holes were like tuxedoed gents in a ball, Wheeler said, spinning women in white gowns. In a dark room the men would seem to disappear, but we would know they were there by the motions of their twirling partners. To find a black hole, Wheeler explained, astronomers needed to find a binary star system—two stars locked in orbit around each other.

In December of 1970, astronomers did just that. The X-ray satellite Uhuru located a blue star twenty-three times the size of our sun in the constellation Cygnus. Every five-and-a-half days it orbited an invisible partner. That partner emitted X-rays, and astronomers calculated it was ten times the mass of our sun. It had to be a black hole. The X-rays were sent out just before matter from the living star was sucked into the black hole's void.

Further examination proved that black holes exist. The larger question was why they act the way they do, and what occurs in those parts that we cannot see. Along the edge of the black hole lies the event horizon. This is the area where the black hole becomes a one-way street. Anything entering its field can only move closer to the singularity.

There is no escape.

Writers and filmmakers have imagined what entering this singularity would be like. Scientists have speculated as well. Perhaps a black hole's singularity was a portal to another dimension, a doorway back in time or across galaxies.

Sadly, it appears the truth is more gruesome. Anyone unfortunate enough to approach a black hole would be caught in the object's gravitational pull. As they approached its singularity, the victim would be stretched into the world's largest noodle. Eventually, all such objects would be infinitely long and have a width of zero.

To Hawking, the most fascinating part of a black hole was not the possibility of using it for intergalactic travel but the idea that nothing could escape. Even light, it was said, was trapped inside the gravitationally collapsed star. Hawking wondered if anything could defy the boundaries of the black hole.

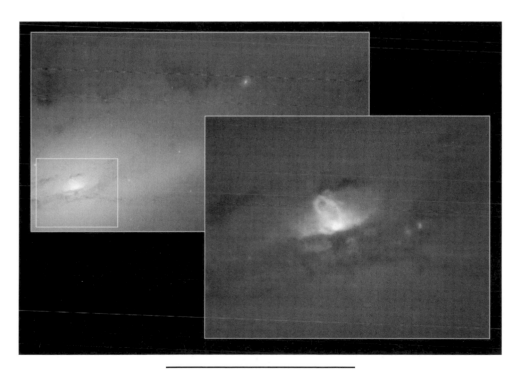

Images of a black hole, as seen through the Hubble Space Telescope.

By now he was the father of two small children—Robert, born in 1967, and Lucy, born three years later. After Robert's birth, Jane commented, "It obviously gave Stephen a great new impetus, being responsible for this tiny creature."[4]

Despite the challenges of his disability, Hawking played an active role in his children's lives. It was not always easy for him or his wife.

"When I married him I knew there was not going to be the possibility of my having a career, that our household could only accommodate one career and that had to be Stephen's."[5] As the children grew older, Jane was able to go back to school, eventually earning a Ph.D. and working as a teacher in Cambridge.

Meanwhile, Hawking's career was exploding like the big bang he described. Once, during the long and difficult process of getting ready for bed (which he refused help with until there was absolutely no alternative), he began developing a new theory about black holes. "The rays of light that form the event horizon, the boundary of the black hole can never approach each other," he later explained. "Consequently, the area of the event horizon (i.e., the black hole surface) might stay the same or increase with time, but it could never decrease."[6] This theory, developed while he put on his pajamas, became known as "Hawking's law of area increase."

Hawking's work was studied by a Princeton student named Jacob Bekenstein. He theorized "that the area of the event horizon was a measure of the entropy of the black hole."[7]

Entropy means *disorder* or *randomness* and is part of the second law of thermodynamics. Thermodynamics, the study of heat and its transformation into mechanical energy, includes three basic laws. The first describes how energy can be transferred from one system to another but can never be created or destroyed. The third looks at "absolute zero," the temperature the universe will reach once all energy and matter is randomly distributed across it.

However, it was the second law's implications that fascinated Bekenstein. This law says that "the entropy of a system can only stay the same or increase but never decrease." If a house is left unrepaired it eventually falls apart. If an egg is dropped on the floor and breaks, it will not "unscramble."

Bekenstein suggested a way that matter pulled into a black hole would create entropy.

There was just one problem.

"In a paper I wrote with Brandon Carter, we pointed out a fatal flaw in Bekenstein's idea," Hawking later said. "If black holes have an entropy, they ought to have a temperature. And if they have a temperature, they ought to give off radiation. But how could they give off radiation if nothing can escape from a black hole?"[8]

The answer arrived during a meeting in Moscow. Hawking visited Yakov Zeldovitch, who was known in Russia as the father of the hydrogen bomb (in the United States, Edward Teller has this honor). Zeldovitch suggested a way that particles might escape from a black hole.

When Hawking returned to Cambridge, he began to rework his mathematics. A moment of clarity came in the middle of a celebratory dinner for his thirty-second birthday. When Roger Penrose called, Hawking began discussing his new theory.

The food grew cold as the two scientists debated the possibilities for nearly an hour. What if the extreme gravity in a black hole created tiny charged particles? These particles usually come in pairs, combining rapidly into gravitational energy. In a black hole, could the tremendous pressure cause one of them to fly away from the other, thrown into space?

It seemed to contradict Hawking's law of increase. Even more stunning, it suggested a way that black holes could gradually diminish, ending their lives in a final, violent explosion equal to over one million hydrogen bombs!

In February of 1974, Hawking offered this new theory in a presentation he called "Black Hole Explosions?" Many of his fellow scientists were convinced he had made a mistake. After his speech, John Taylor, the session's chairman, said, "I'm sorry, Stephen, but this is absolute rubbish."[9] Hawking wrote a paper explaining his theory for the respected science journal *Nature*. Taylor wrote his own article, attempting to disprove Hawking's theories.

"However, in the end most people, including John Taylor, have come to the conclusion that black holes must radiate like hot bodies if our other ideas about general relativity and quantum mechanics are correct."[10]

By then Hawking had published his first book, *The Large-Scale Structure of Space-Time*, which he wrote with George Ellis. Even cosmologists had a hard time understanding it. On a train ride, radio astronomer John Shakeshift confessed, "I thought I might make it to page 10, but I only got as far as page 4, and I've given up, I'm afraid!"[11]

Hawking's work earned him induction into The Royal Society. Becoming one of the youngest members of England's most respected scientific organizations was an incredible honor. Many of the members had won Nobel Prizes. Even Sir Isaac Newton once belonged.

At the time Hawking was inducted, accommodations for physically challenged people were not very common. At the society there was not a wheelchair ramp, and Hawking could not get onto the stage. Instead, the book that new members sign was brought down to him. Carefully, slowly, he scrawled his signature.

Hawking was losing the use of his hands. More and more, he had to remember complex equations, rather than writing them down.

". . . Because the loss of control over his hands was so gradual, Hawking has had plenty of time to adapt," former student Kip Thorne once pointed out. " He has gradually trained his mind to think in a manner different from that of the minds of other physicists."[12]

Instead of drawing pictures or writing pages of long calculations, Hawking used his head. He would need his mind more as his body weakened and the theories he once championed suddenly seemed wrong.

A New Beginning

THE CATHOLIC CHURCH ARRESTED Galileo for his work. Over three hundred years later, the Church offered Stephen Hawking a prize for his. In the 1600s, the church believed Galileo's writing questioned God's place in the universe. By the 1900s, the Church thought that Hawking's big bang research proved the existence of a divine creator. In 1979, they honored the cosmologist with the Pope Pius XI Gold Medal.

"I was in two minds whether to accept, because of Galileo," Hawking later admitted. "When I arrived in Rome to receive the award, I insisted on being shown the record of Galileo's trial in the Vatican library."[1]

The Catholic Church had been supportive of the big bang theory before it even got its name, back in 1951 when they acknowledged Abbe George LeMaitre's cosmic egg theory as evidence of God. Hawking was not so sure. He often viewed religion as he viewed astrology and ESP, a poor excuse for people who did not want to put in the effort to understand physics. The big bang did not prove or disprove the hand of God.

In April of 1979, Hawking received an even greater honor. The university he had taught at for well over a decade, Cambridge University, named him the Lucasian Professor of Mathematics. It was the same position once held by Sir Isaac Newton.

Every Lucasian professor gives a special lecture in honor of the appointment. However, by then Hawking's speech was so slurred that only his closest colleagues and friends could understand him. The boy who had once spoken "Hawkingnese" had grown into a man who could no longer communicate directly with a classroom.

It did not really matter. Hawking was able to get this point across by having a graduate student read the lecture he had prepared. "Is the End in Sight for Theoretical Physics" was nearly as controversial as his theory about black hole radiation. Theoretical physics attempts to explain how portions of the universe behave. Hawking believed that someday soon all of the properties of physics would be understood and proven—thus, there would be no more need for "theory."

The same year he became Lucasian professor, Stephen and Jane had another son, Timothy. By now Hawking himself needed constant care, a step the scientist resisted. He hated to have others take care of him. Jane could do only so much, however. Beginning in 1974, the Hawkings began inviting research students to live with them and help Hawking out. They were given free room and board in exchange, but even more valuable was the opportunity to ask questions of the cosmologist. It seemed like a fair trade, although Hawking later admitted, "It was hard for a student to be in awe of his professor after he has helped him to the bathroom."[2]

The ALS continued to progress, and Hawking had to abandon a special car fitted for his disability and rely on a motorized wheelchair. Still, a reporter once wrote, "At full throttle the chair is capable of a decent trotting pace, and Hawking likes to use full throttle. He also knows no fear."[3]

Despite his worsening condition, Hawking continued to re-examine his theories. During a second visit to the Vatican in 1981, he began questioning the idea that won him Church support: the singularity of the big bang. Beginning the universe with a singularity (and concluding it in the same way) was always a problem for mathematicians like Roger Penrose, because a singularity has infinite density and zero size. Zero can not be properly divided, and mathematicians are not fond of "infinities."

The Vatican Garden, St. Peter's, in Rome, Italy.

Physicists are not too fond of singularities, either. At this mathematical point, all of the laws of physics fall apart.

Along with fellow scientist James Hoyle, Hawking set out to solve this dilemma. In 1983, the two presented a new theory. It included the big bang and the big crunch, but this time there was no singularity. Instead, the universe compressed into a tiny space but afterwards, expanded after an enormous explosion, long before zeros or infinities applied.

To some, this "no boundary proposal" called into question the need for a "creator." Many saw the big bang as the Catholic Church did, as a cosmic light switch waiting to be flicked on by a higher power. A never-ending cycle of big bangs and big crunches meant there was no such need.

"All that my work has shown is that you don't have to say that the way the universe began was the personal whim of God. But you still have the question: Why does the universe bother to exist? If you like, you can define God to be the answer to that question."[4]

This disagreement helped motivate Hawking to write a book. He did not want to write for a few scientists. Instead, he wanted to explain his work to the general public, writing a book they could buy at airports or grocery stores, instead of just college bookshops. " I was excited about the discoveries that have been made in the last twenty-five years, and I wanted to tell people about them."[5]

He also had a practical reason. His daughter was attending an expensive school, paying her tuition on a professor's salary was not easy. A popular book would help him financially.

Hawking sat down and wrote the first chapter. A friend introduced him to a literary agent named Al Zuckerman. Zuckerman's job was to help writers get their books accepted by publishers. The agent liked Hawking's work and began sending the manuscript out in 1984.

A number of publishers liked the work, and Zuckerman suggested that Hawking sign a contract with Norton, a respected publisher of "upmarket" books written for an elite audience.

Instead, Hawking decided to write for Bantam. Bantam's books were sold in airports. That is where Hawking wanted to be.

The publisher wanted a complete revision to make the book understandable to people who were not scientists. Hawking began a re-write. Then, in 1985 his voice was almost silenced forever.

The Brief History

WATCHING TELEVISION IN THE EARLY 1980s, millions of viewers were fascinated by the PBS program *Cosmos*. Hosted by Carl Sagan, a Cornell University professor and author, it introduced numerous discoveries in astronomy. It also explained how the work of scientists affected life on earth. The show led many to buy the book of the same name. *Cosmos* became the best-selling science book ever published in the English language.

Stephen Hawking believed the audience for *Cosmos* would be just as interested in his book, *A Brief History of Time*. The public's fascination with black holes continued. Whenever a newspaper or a television program did a piece on them, Hawking was the first person they interviewed. People began to recognize him on the street. But he did not write the book to become famous. He wrote it to make hard-to-understand concepts understandable. He wrote as he thought, using word pictures instead of mathematical equations. He imagined his readers as the same people who would have a hard time getting past page ten of his first book.

By 1985, Hawking was doing revisions of his book for Peter Guzzardi, his editor at Bantam. Guzzardi was very demanding. Every time Hawking sent him a rewritten chapter, Guzzardi sent it back, along with lists of questions and a request to do it again. In July, Hawking moved into a small house in Geneva, Switzerland, hoping to escape the distractions of Cambridge.

The move almost killed him.

One night his personal nurse came in to check on him. Something was wrong. Hawking's face was a bright purple—he could not breathe.

The cosmologist was rushed to the hospital. Hawking had pneumonia, a very serious lung inflammation. Many of those weakened by ALS die when they catch pneumonia. They are not strong enough to breathe once their lungs are infected, and they slowly suffocate.

Stephen Hawking was dying.

There was only one option: an emergency tracheotomy. This operation creates an air passage through the larynx (the "voice box") in the throat. The surgery could save Hawking's life.

It would also take away his voice. He was not awake to make the decision—it was up to his wife. "It was my decision for him to have [a tracheotomy]," Jane later admitted. "But I have sometimes thought, what have I done? What sort of life have I let him in for?"[1]

When Hawking emerged from the operation, he could communicate only by having a person point to letters on a card. He would raise his eyebrows when the correct one was pointed out. It was an impossibly slow way to communicate.

There did not seem to be any chance he would finish working on his book.

Once again, however, technology altered Hawking's life. Advances in computers would give him a new voice. Software engineer Walt Woltosz heard about Hawking's challenge and got in touch with the cosmologist. His California company, Words Plus, had a program that could help him and that would work on the computer attached to Hawking's wheelchair.

Once installed, Hawking was able to use the device to "speak." Although his condition left him movement of a few fingers only, he could scroll down a list and touch the screen when he reached the right word. There were three thousand to choose from. Once selected, the word would be spoken through a voice synthesizer. Hawking would be able to continue to lecture at schools and talk to his family.

He would also be able to finish his book.

A Brief History of Time was published in 1988. It came out on April 1st, but its success was no April Fool's Day joke. With an introduction by

Stephen Hawking demonstrates his notebook computer—specially modified for him by Intel engineers—for Intel chairman Gordon Moore.

Carl Sagan, the book set out to explain cosmology and other scientific principles from their beginnings a few thousand years ago up to the present.

The book was an immediate hit. It stayed on the London Times bestseller list for 237 weeks— longer than any other book. Earning a mention in the *Guinness Book of World Records*, the book did equally well in the United States, where it was a *New York Times* bestseller for over a year. It was translated into over three-dozen languages. Estimates suggest that the book has been purchased by 1 out of every 750 people on the planet!

Hawking knows quite a few people buy it to show off, leaving it unread on a bookshelf or a coffee table as evidence of how smart they are. However, the thousands of detailed questions he has received from people from all walks of life prove that many who buy it, read it.

Hawking became famous. He appeared in an episode of *Star Trek: The Next Generation* playing poker with Albert Einstein and Sir Issac Newton. He also "appeared" on the cartoon *The Simpsons*, animated alongside Bart, Lisa, and all the rest.

"I'm sure my disability has a bearing on why I'm well known," Hawking says on his Web site. "People are fascinated by the contrast between my very limited physical powers and the vast nature of the universe I deal with."[2]

Stephen Hawking looks on during a public lecture in 2001 while the large monitor plays a clip of his guest appearance on an episode of The Simpsons.

Sadly, his own universe was harder to deal with. In 1990, he and his wife separated. Some have said the divorce was the result of the increased level of care he required after his tracheotomy; others because of disagreements over religion. Hawking has refused to speak publicly about the end of his first marriage. Five years later he would marry Elaine Mason, who had been his nurse.

The success of Hawking's book has not kept him from the challenges of cosmology. Albert Einstein spent his final years working on a unified field theory, a theory to predict all of the behaviors of the universe. Einstein failed in this

Stephen Hawking and his second wife, Elaine, on their wedding day in September 1995.

quest. Hawking and his colleagues mounted a similar exploration. They called it TOE, *the theory of everything*. Scientists believe that by understanding how everything from the smallest particle to the largest galaxy behaves, they can almost predict the future.

Some think that understanding the universe in this way means eventually controlling it. By 2003, Hawking had changed his mind. In a January lecture at Cambridge he said, "Some people will be very disappointed if there is not an ultimate theory that can be formulated as a finite number of principles. I used to belong to that camp, but I have changed my mind. I'm now glad that our search for understanding will never come to an end, and that we will always have the challenge in new discovery."[3]

Not long after, Hawking would change his mind regarding another issue in physics. For years, Hawking had insisted that information about what falls into a black hole could never be retrieved. But at a scientific conference in Dublin in July 2004, he reversed himself, declaring that such information could indeed be recovered.

"If you jump into a black hole," he said, "your mass energy will be returned to our universe, but in a mangled form, which contains the information about what you were like, but in an unrecognizable state."[4]

Despite the challenges in his life, he feels the discoveries have been worth it. Over sixty years ago, Lou Gehrig told his fans that he felt lucky. Stephen Hawking feels the same way.

"I have been very fortunate in everything except getting motor neuron disease," he told author Joseph P. McEvoy in 1994. "And even the disease has not been such a blow. With a lot of help, I have managed to get round the effects. I have the satisfaction in having succeeded in spite of it. I'm really much happier than I was before it began. I can't say it has been a benefit, but I have been lucky that it has not been the disadvantage it could have been."[5]

Activities

Theoretical physics relies on often-complex equations and formulas to explain the universe. Yet, some very simple experiments can give you a better idea of how stars behave and the effect of space curvature on planets.

Activity One: Black Holes

Black holes are created when a very large star runs out of fuel and collapses. If a large star and a small star are an equal distance away from earth, the largest star will also appear the brightest. A simple experiment shows how this works.

You will need:

- Aluminum foil
- Scissors
- Blank paper
- A flashlight

Tear off a square of aluminum foil, and fold it

in half. Use the scissors to carefully cut a small oval from the center of the folded section. Unfold. Wrap the foil over the end of the flashlight so that the hole is placed over the lens. Enter a darkened room with the flashlight and the sheet of paper.

Set down the paper. Now, aim the flashlight beam at the paper. Notice what happens?

Next, remove the aluminum foil from the flashlight and aim the beam at the paper again.

Reducing the area of the flashlight's beam also reduces the circle of brightness. The smaller the star, the less bright it is.

However, a close small star will appear brighter than a distant large one.

Activity Two: Gravitational Pressure

Black holes are formed when a star several times the size of the sun collapses. It collapses because its mass is so great that gravitational forces overwhelm it once fuel has run out, reducing the black hole to a singularity.

You cannot create a singularity, but you can see how gravitational pressure can cause a star to collapse.

You will need:

- Two balloons
- Two large cups or jars

Place the balloons in the cups so that the ends are still outside. Blow up the balloons inside the cups, and then knot the ends. Place one cup in the freezer and leave the other one out. Wait for one hour.

Next, remove the cup from the freezer. Do you see what has happened? The balloon has shrunk, while the one left outside is about the same size. In the freezer the pressure inside the balloon in not equal to the pressure outside and so the balloon shrinks.

Activity Three: Curvature of Space

Albert Einstein discussed the effect of the curvature of space on large bodies. With a few friends you can imitate this effect.

You will need:

- A blanket or sheet
- A basketball
- Several tennis balls
- A few friends

Have your friends hold the blanket tightly outstretched. Now, toss the basketball onto the sheet. Follow it with the tennis balls. Notice how the smaller balls move towards the larger one. See how the blanket has curved? This experiment shows the way space curves, affecting the large and small bodies that move through it.

Chronology

300s B.C.—The first cosmologist, Aristotle, presents theories about the stars and planets.

1543—Copernicus's *On the Revolutions of the Heavenly Spheres* is published, a book detailing his model of a sun-centered universe; Copernicus dies this same year.

1642—Galileo Galilei dies after being sentenced to house arrest by the Roman Inquisition.

1665—Twenty-four-year-old Isaac Newton crafts his laws of gravity, space, and time.

1670—Speed of light is determined by Danish astronomer Olaus Roemer using the eclipses of Jupiter's moons.

1887—Edward Morley and Albert Abraham Michelson show light's speed is constant.

1905—Einstein publishes his theories of special relativity showing how the speed of light affects time.

1916—Einstein publishes his "General Theory of Relativity" proposing that our sun caused the space around it to curve, thus explaining Earth's movement through space.

1919—During a solar eclipse A.C.D. Crommelin's and Arthur Eddington's star photos show light is bent, proving Einstein's theory.

1942—Stephen William Hawking is born on

January 8, in Oxford, England, to Frank and Isobel Hawking.

1952—Begins studies at St. Alban's School.

1959—Enters Oxford University as physics major.

1962—Begins studies at Cambridge University towards a doctorate in cosmology.

1965—Marries Jane Wilde; earns his Ph.D. from Cambridge.

1965—Arno Penzias and Robert Wilson discover cosmic background radiation.

1969—John Wheeler first calls gravitationally collapsed stars "black holes."

1970—Stephen Hawking begins study, that leads to his law of area increase.

1974—Presents his theory about black hole explosions.

1979—Awarded the Pope Pius XI Gold Medal from the Catholic Church.

1981—Re-examines idea that big bangs and big crunches begins with a singularity.

1985—Loses voice as a result of tracheotomy; given a computerized speech synthesizer for communications.

1988—*A Brief History of Time* is published; it becomes one of the best selling books ever.

1990—Separates from Jane.

1990s—Explores TOE theory, the theory of everything.

1995—Marries his nurse, Elaine Mason.

2003—Discusses why science may never provide a theory to cover everything in the universe.

Chapter Notes

Chapter 1. A Lucky Man

1. Michael White and John Stephen Gribbin, *Stephen Hawking: A Life in Science* (New York: Dutton, 1992), p. 60.

2. T. J. Quinn, "Luckiest Man on the Face of the Earth," *New York Daily News*, April 15, 2003, p. 8.

Chapter 2. Controversy

1. Stephen Hawking, ed., *A Brief History of Time: A Reader's Companion* (New York: Bantam Books, 1992), p. 4.

2. Ibid.

3. Stephen Hawking, *Black Holes and Baby Universes and Other Essays* (New York: Bantam Books, 1993), p. 9.

4. Stephen Hawking, ed., *A Brief History of Time: A Reader's Companion*, p. 21.

5. Ibid., p. 13.

6. Ibid., p. 25.

7. Michael White and John Stephen Gribbin, *Stephen Hawking: A Life in Science* (New York: Dutton, 1992), pp. 14–15.

8. Ibid., p. 20.

Chapter 3. A Lazy Student?

1. Stephen, Hawking, ed., *A Brief History of Time: A Reader's Companion* (New York: Bantam Books, 1992), p. 37.

2. Ibid.

3. David Filkin, *Stephen Hawking's Universe: The Cosmos Explained* (New York: Harper Collins, 1997), p. 3.

4. Stephen Hawking, *Black Holes and Baby Universes and Other Essays* (New York: Bantam Books, 1993), p. 14.

5. Ibid., p. 15.

Chapter 4. Cosmic Eggs and Big Bangs

1. "Newton's Birth Date and the Anni Mirabiles," n.d., <http://www.mathpages.com/home/kmath121.htm> (March 10, 2004).

2. Stephen Hawking, *A Brief History of Time: Updated and Expanded Tenth Anniversary Edition* (New York: Bantam Books, 1998), p. 85.

3. J. P. McEvoy and Oscar Zarate, *Introducing Stephen Hawking* (Cambridge: Icon Books, 1999), p. 68.

4. Stephen Hawking, ed., *A Brief History of Time: A Reader's Companion* (New York: Bantam Books, 1992), p. 53.

5. McEvoy and Zarate, pp. 70–71.

Chapter 5. The Beginning of Time

1. Stephen Hawking, ed., *A Brief History of Time: A Reader's Companion* (New York: Bantam Books, 1992), p. 55.

2. Michael White and John Stephen Gribbin, *Stephen Hawking: A Life in Science* (New York: Dutton, 1992), p. 72.

3. Stephen Hawking, ed., *A Brief History of Time: A Reader's Companion* (New York: Bantam Books, 1992), pp. 54–55.

Chapter 6. The Big and the Small of It

1. Stephen Hawking, ed., *A Brief History of Time: A Reader's Companion* (New York: Bantam Books, 1992), pp. 72–73.

2. J. P. McEvoy and Oscar Zarate, *Introducing Stephen Hawking* (Cambridge: Icon Books, 1999), p. 97.

3. Ibid., p. 102.

Chapter 7. Black Holes and White Dwarfs

1. J. P. McEvoy and Oscar Zarate, *Introducing Stephen Hawking* (Cambridge: Icon Books, 1999), p. 109.

2. Ibid.

3. Ibid.

4. Michael White and John Stephen Gribbin, *Stephen Hawking: A Life in Science* (New York: Dutton, 1992), p. 99.

5. Ibid., p. 99.

6. McEvoy and Zarate, p. 125.

7. Stephen Hawking, *A Brief History of Time: Updated and Expanded Tenth Anniversary Edition* (New York: Bantam Books, 1998), p. 107.

8. Stephen Hawking, ed., *A Brief History of Time: A Reader's Companion* (New York: Bantam Books, 1992), p. 95.

9. McEvoy and Zarate, p. 141.

10. Stephen Hawking, *A Brief History of Time: Updated and Expanded Tenth Anniversary Edition* (New York: Bantam Books, 1998), p. 116.

11. White and Gribbin, p. 128.

12. McEvoy and Zarate, pp. 122–123.

Chapter 8. A New Beginning

1. J. P. McEvoy and Oscar Zarate, *Introducing Stephen Hawking* (Cambridge: Icon Books, 1999), p. 150.

2. Michael White and John Stephen Gribbin, *Stephen Hawking: A Life in Science* (New York: Dutton, 1992), p. 158.

3. Ibid., p. 160.

4. Stephen Hawking, *Black Holes and Baby Universes and Other Essays* (New York: Bantam Books, 1993), p. 173.

5. Ibid., p. 169.

Chapter 9. The Brief History

1. Michael White and John Stephen Gribbin, *Stephen Hawking: A Life in Science* (New York: Dutton, 1992), p. 234.

2. *Stephen Hawking Website*, n.d., <http://www.hawking.org.uk/info/news.html> (March 10, 2004).

3. Cambridge lecture, n.d., <http://www.cambridge-mit.org/cgi-bin/default> (March 10, 2004).

4. Dennis Overbye, "About Those Fearsome Black Holes? Never Mind," *The New York Times*, July 22, 2004, p. A3.

5. J. P. McEvoy and Oscar Zarate, *Introducing Stephen Hawking* (Cambridge: Icon Books, 1999), p. 49.

Glossary

absolute motion—Motion that does not change no matter what system it is measured in. (Does not exist.)

absolute time—Time that does not change regardless of an observer's motion in the universe. (Does not exist.)

acceleration—Rate of change of velocity.

cosmology—The study of the universe as a whole.

entropy—A measure of disorder or randomness in a system.

gravity—The attractive force generated by an object because of its mass.

heresy—An opinion that conflicts with a religious belief.

implosion—An inward collapse.

inertia—Resistance to change or motion.

mass—The amount of matter in an object.

matter—Something that occupies space and displays properties of gravity.

physics—Science of matter and energy and the interactions between them.

psuedoscience—False science.

weight—Force exerted on a body by a gravitational field.

Further Reading

Cole, Ron. *Stephen Hawking: Solving the Mysteries of the Universe*. Austin, Tex.: Raintree/Steck-Vaughn Publishers, 1998.

Cropper, William H. *Great Physicists: The Life and Times of Leading Physicists from Galileo to Hawking*. New York: Oxford University Press, 2001.

Ferguson, Kitty. *Stephen Hawking: Quest for a Theory of the Universe*. New York: Bantam Books, 1992.

McDaniel, Melissa. *Stephen Hawking: Revolutionary Physicist*. Broomall, Pa.: Chelsea House Publishers, 1994.

Sakurai, Gail. *Stephen Hawking: Understanding the Universe*. Danbury, Conn.: Children's Press, 1996.

Internet Addresses

Professor Stephen W. Hawking's Web Pages
http://www.hawking.org.uk/home/hindex.html

Virtual Trips to Black Holes and Neutron Stars
http://antwrp.gsfc.nasa.gov/htmltest/rjn_bht.html

Falling Into a Black Hole
http://casa.colorado.edu/~ajsh/schw.shtml

Index